Listen to your

SMART VOICE!

And Stay Safe!

[a child safety manual for children]

by

Sharon Nemeth Murch

For information about Smart Voice child safety programs
for use in schools or community events

or for bulk purchases

please contact:

SMART VOICE Child Safety
P.O. Box 55844
Hayward, CA 94540

e-mail
missingmichaela@gmail.com

A very important note for Parents
and other Trusted Grown-Ups

There is no way you can absolutely guarantee the safety of your child. You can educate them all the live-long day, but chances are those who want to hurt children will think up something you haven't thought to tell them about. My daughter, Michaela, had been through two different child safety training programs in school, and I had talked to her at home extensively on the subject in the aftermath of two abductions in our area, which had occurred just months before Michaela was kidnapped. But nobody had never thought to say, "If your scooter is not where you left it, don't go and get it." So one day when that happened, she did go to get it, and a man jumped out of the car next to the scooter, grabbed her from behind, threw her into his car, and took off with her. She has never been found.

I have thought to include that scenario and similar ones in this booklet, and many others. There is a lot of information in here, and it may be difficult for a child to digest all in one sitting. It is something that should be read over and reinforced over time. Discuss these concepts with your child in everyday life. Practice them. Based on your child's maturity level, when you are out with them, ask them, "If that person over there did this, what would you do?" Show your kids how to perform some of the tasks discussed in this book, like removing car keys. And if there is anything I have said in this book that you don't agree with, tell your child. Sometimes it takes risky behavior to escape from dangerous situations. I sat and discussed these things with the police and FBI agents assigned to my daughter's kidnapping case, and they agreed with my suggestions. But I do actually suggest the possibility of trying to cause a car accident if they are being kidnapped. I fully recognize the dangers of causing an accident while you are in the car, but the consensus of opinion seems to be that it may be the child's last best chance. It is rare that a child returns from a stranger abduction. But you talk to your child, and if you disagree with this, then tell him or her.

I do believe that all children have a SMART VOICE. I believe that this SMART VOICE can be educated and made even smarter, but I believe that half the battle is just making kids aware of it, and teaching them to listen to it instead of panicking in a dangerous situation, or instead of giving in to dangerous behavior in a tempting situation.

One thing that comes up with child safety programs is parents' concerns about frightening their children. It is my experience that most children are not frightened. In fact, most children seem to feel some sense of invulnerability. Even my own children, knowing the reality of kidnapping, were quick to tell me that if somebody tried to kidnap them, they would "just kick him." Just a little bit of fear is a healthy thing. And it can save lives. Kidnapping is not something that happens only in bad dreams, or to other people's kids, or on the 5:00 news. It is very real. It can happen to your child.

More than anything, however, I would hope that this kind of child safety education is empowering, not frightening. Yes, there is danger, but no, you are not powerless. Children need to be taught to be strong, to be smart. They need to be taught that they don't always have to be obedient and compliant.

This book comes from my heart. I pray no child who ever reads this book, or has it read to him or her, will ever need the lessons within it. But if even one child is able to come home safely because she listened to her Smart Voice, it will be to me a blessing beyond measure.

God bless and stay safe,

Sharon Nemeth Murch
Michaela Joy Garecht's mom

This book is dedicated to my daughter,
MICHAELA JOY GARECHT

You are always in my heart.
I believe you will yet again be in my arms.

Okay …

Almost everyone has heard that, if you want to stay safe,
you have to follow the basic rule …

*DON'T TALK TO
STRANGERS!*

This is good advice. But then the question is,

**WHO IS A
STRANGER?**

Often we think of strangers as people we don't know. And that is one definition
of a stranger. Most of those people aren't dangerous, and some of them might
even be helpful, or might become our friends if we get to know them.

But you don't know that when you first meet them. Especially if the stranger is older than you, you should be cautious unless you are with a Trusted Grown-Up.

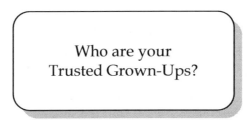

Who are your
Trusted Grown-Ups?

Every child has Trusted Grown-Ups in his or her life. Usually these include your mom or dad, maybe your grandparents or your babysitter, your teacher or principal or the yard duty at school, maybe your doctor. You know who these people are because you have known them for awhile. They take care of you. They make you feel safe. These are the people you should go to whenever you have any doubts or questions.

Some strangers can be dangerous.

That is a Stranger with a capital "S"!

What makes him (or her) a Stranger is that he has a bad heart. Not the kind of bad heart that your grandpa takes pills for. The kind of bad heart that is full of bad thoughts.

This makes it hard to identify a Stranger, because you usually can't see a person's heart if they don't want you to.

It is very difficult to identify a Stranger by the way he or she looks.

A stranger may be ugly and scary looking.
Or a stranger might be cool looking and attractive.
A stranger might act mean.
Or a stranger might seem really nice and friendly.

A Stranger can be
young or old,
a man or a woman,
pretty or ugly,
cool or nerdy,
mean or nice,
strong or weak.

Sometimes, a Stranger will change the way he or she looks or acts in order to fool you, so that you will think they are nice when they are not.

Usually we think of strangers as someone we don't know, but the really scary thing is that *sometimes* a Stranger might even be someone we know, someone we have seen often, someone we have spoken to.

So we are back to that question:

HOW DO WE KNOW IF A PERSON IS A STRANGER?

We all have voices inside us that help us think, and help us decide what to do.

One of those voices might be called your I WANT voice. This is the voice that speaks up whenever we see something that we want. It doesn't care if what we want might be bad for us, or dangerous, or too expensive, or against the rules. It doesn't think about the future, or the consequences of our actions. It just wants what it wants, and it usually wants it right now.

Another of those voices might be called our AFRAID voice. This voice might make us afraid even when we don't need to be. It might make us think that there is something under the bed, even when we know there isn't. It might make us afraid to do things that would really be good for us.

It is okay to want things, and there are times when it is okay to be afraid also, but these voices don't know the difference between when it's okay and when it's not.

So in order to figure that out, we have to learn to shush those voices, and listen instead to our SMART VOICE.

I can be SMART!

Our SMART VOICE takes time to think about things. It thinks not just about the present moment, but also about the future. It thinks, "If I do this, what is likely to happen?" and "If I *don't* do this, what is likely to happen?"

You are probably already pretty familiar with these voices.

For example:

Your ball rolls out into the street, and a car is coming. Your I WANT voice tells you to get right out there and get it because it is your favorite ball and your I WANT voice wants that ball and doesn't want it to get squished. But your SMART VOICE tells you that if you do that, it might be you that gets squished instead of the ball, and that would hurt. Your SMART VOICE tells you that you can always get another ball, but you can't get another you, and you are way more valuable than a ball, even if it is your favorite one.

Your I WANT voice tells you that you want to sit and play video games all day, but your SMART VOICE tells you that if you do that, you won't get your homework done. And it tells you that even though you might have more fun today, tomorrow in school you will feel dumb when you don't have your homework to turn in, and you might even get in trouble and lose a recess, and way down the road you might get bad grades, and you might even lose out on a *whole summer* of video games, and playing with your friends, because you will have to go to summer school because you played video games all day instead of doing your homework.

Your SMART VOICE also tells you things like not to touch the stove when something is cooking on it, because you might get burned. It tells you that a bear might look soft and cuddly, but you should stay away from it anyway because the bear probably isn't going to feel the same way about you, and its teeth are very big and very sharp!

Your SMART VOICE tells you things all the time, and they may not always seem like the most fun things. But it's really a good idea to practice listening to your SMART VOICE and doing what it says, so you will recognize it in situations where the right thing and the wrong thing might not be quite so clear, and where the dangers might be very bad.

Like figuring out WHO IS A STRANGER.

Then there is the AFRAID voice. That voice might tell you that there is a monster under your bed, or in the closet. But your SMART VOICE will tell you that you have looked under your bed many times, and you open your closet every day, and there are not any monsters there. Your SMART VOICE will tell you that you will be way better off closing your eyes and getting some sleep than lying awake worrying about something that you really know is not there.

Your AFRAID voice might also make you afraid to try out for a sports team, or to audition for a part in the school play, or to sing in front of people. But your SMART VOICE will look ahead and say, "Hey, what's the worst that could happen?" If you messed up, you'd be embarrassed for a minute, and maybe you wouldn't be on the team or in the play. But if you don't try, you for sure won't be on the team or in the play. On the other hand, your SMART VOICE will be able to look ahead, and it will be able to see how much fun you will have if you do get on the team, or into the play, and it will tell you that is well worth facing your fear to try out. And who knows? Maybe you are really a star just waiting to be discovered!

You might have already figured it out, but if you ever have trouble figuring out which is your SMART VOICE, it might help you to know that *sometimes* your SMART VOICE sounds just a little bit like a mom…. But that's good! Doesn't it feel good to know that you can be as bright as a mom?

I'm so smart!

Staying Safe

So what might your SMART VOICE tell you about how to keep safe from Strangers?

Well, first of all, it will tell you to listen to your Trusted Grown-Ups. If your Trusted Grown-Ups tell you that they don't want you to do something, or go somewhere, it is not because they don't want you to have any fun. They love you after all, and they really want you to be happy! But sometimes they have to say no, because they are trying to keep you safe.

Your SMART VOICE will also tell you that when you go outside to play, or to walk to the park or the store (with permission, of course), you should never go alone. You should always go with someone else. It doesn't have to be a Trusted Grown-Up. It can be a friend your age. A Stranger is more likely to bother a child who is alone than one who is with a friend.

> This is called the
> BUDDY SYSTEM!

If you walk to and from school, you should use the Buddy System also. And after school, if you walk home without a parent or Trusted Grown-Up, you should leave immediately when the bell rings, and go right home. This is safer because there are usually lots of kids and their parents walking home right after school gets out, but if you hang around too long everyone else will be gone and you will be walking alone. If your teacher keeps your class after school, have your parents talk to your principal about this, because it really is important to your safety.

If you are going somewhere (with the permission of your Trusted Grown-Ups and with your Buddy), always go the same way, and make sure your Trusted Grown-Ups know which way that is in case they need to find you.

Also, if you listen to your SMART VOICE, it will tell you to stay away from strange places where nobody can see you. Don't go into alleyways or behind strange buildings, or into strange buildings, or cars. Try to stay in places where lots of people will be driving and walking by and will be able to see you.

Strangers are less likely to bother you in those places.

So what might your SMART VOICE tell you in some specific situations?

Let's think about it ….

What if ...

Someone you don't know comes up to you and says that he has lost his puppy, and he wants you to help look for it.

One of your voices, one that loves animals and wants to help people, will probably say, "Oh, poor puppy! It might be getting hungry, or it might be cold, or it might be scared, or it might get run over by a car, so I should help to save that puppy!" Now that is a very nice voice, but you really need to stop and listen to your SMART VOICE.

Your SMART VOICE will say,

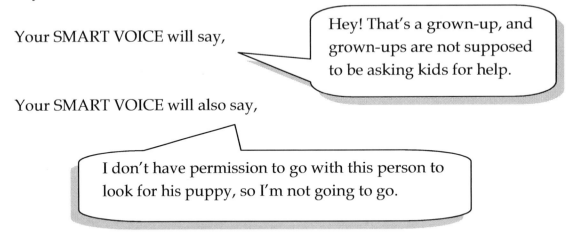

Hey! That's a grown-up, and grown-ups are not supposed to be asking kids for help.

Your SMART VOICE will also say,

I don't have permission to go with this person to look for his puppy, so I'm not going to go.

You should listen to your SMART VOICE.

If the person really has a lost puppy, he really doesn't need you to help find it. He can find it himself, or there are lots of other people who are grown-ups who can help him.

So your SMART VOICE will tell you *not* to go with the person to look for the puppy.

But what will it tell you that you *should* do?

Your SMART VOICE will tell you to find one of your Trusted Grown-Ups and tell them. That way if the grown-up really needs help, he will get it. And if the grown-up is really a Stranger with bad things in his heart, he can be stopped before he finds a child who will not listen to his SMART VOICE.

Hey, mom, you know what happened?

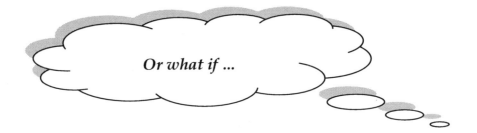

Or what if ...

A Stranger tells you that he has a box of puppies in the back of his car, and asks if you want to see them?

Or he asks if you want an ice cream?

Or he says he wants to give you a toy, or a video game, or anything else he would know a kid would like to have?

Yeah, you can bet that your I WANT voice will be yelling,

"HEY, I WANT THAT!!!!"

It will be telling you to get yourself right over there, because you just love puppies, or ice cream, or toys or video games or whatever it is the Stranger is promising you.

But what would your SMART VOICE be saying? It will yell, really loudly,

STAY AWAY FROM THAT CAR!

This is a very important thing that your SMART VOICE will tell you, always: "STAY AWAY FROM THAT CAR!"

When someone starts trying to get you to get close to them, or to their car, turn around and walk the other way, or better yet, RUN the other way. Find a Trusted Grown-Up, and tell him or her what happened.

But what if ...

You are playing, and you notice that your bicycle or your ball or your doll or your book or your skateboard or your scooter or anything else is not where you left it. What if it has been moved, and it is over next to a car or a building or an area where someone could hide?

DON'T GO GET IT!

Sometimes a Stranger might move something of yours to get you to go close enough to his or her car or house for them to be able to just reach out and grab you.

Go and get a Trusted Grown-Up to help you get it back.

Or what would your SMART VOICE tell you to do if you thought someone was following you? What if you are walking down the street, and there is a car driving along right behind you? Usually cars drive much faster than you can walk, so that would be a very odd thing, and your SMART VOICE would recognize that.

Your SMART VOICE would tell you to turn around and run the other way. It would take a long time for the car to turn around and follow you.

If you are walking and you think someone is following you, you might try walking a little faster, or even running. If the person behind you starts walking faster or running to keep up with you, you will know that they are following you. So if that happens, you are going to have to let your SMART VOICE look around you and tell you what you should do next.

> One thing you have to remember is that anytime you are in actual danger from a Stranger, that kind of automatically makes almost everyone else a Trusted Grown-Up.

If you are near a place of business, run inside and yell for help. If you are near houses, run and bang on a front door. Wherever you are, start yelling and screaming as loudly as you can. Strangers don't like noise, because they don't want anybody to see them doing their Stranger things, because they don't want to get caught and go to jail.

Sometimes making enough noise will make a Stranger just go away.

So remember …

SCREAM AS LOUDLY AS YOU CAN! YELL …

HELP ME!

AND RUN TOWARDS WHEREVER THERE ARE OTHER PEOPLE.

If you should somehow get too close to a Stranger, and they try to grab you and take you away, scream and yell for help.

And don't just scream "aaaaaahhhhhhh!", because sometimes other grown-ups might just think that Stranger is your dad or mom, and you are just being a brat. So if someone grabs you and tries to take you with them, scream as loud as you can,

HELP ME! I'M BEING KIDNAPPED!

Or yell,

THIS IS NOT MY DAD!

Or if you can't get that many words out, scream,

HELP! FIRE!

because that gets people's attention, and that is what you want to do. You want to get people's attention.

But What if ...

A grown-up comes up to you and tells you that something has happened to your mom or dad, or that your dog got run over, or that something else terrible happened?

You would be scared and upset, right? Your voices would not even think, they would just say, "Go, go, go!" because you would be so worried.

But stop, and check to see what your SMART VOICE says.

It can help you recognize your SMART VOICE if you have talked about these things beforehand with your parents. One thing that can help you know when you are listening to your SMART VOICE is having a FAMILY CODE WORD.

> A FAMILY CODE WORD
> is a special word that only
> you and your family
> know, and you have all
> memorized it.

So if ever it is true that something terrible has happened and your parents sent someone to come and get you, they would tell that person the FAMILY CODE WORD so you would know.

You would say,

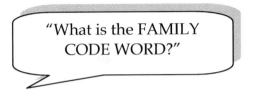

> "What is the FAMILY
> CODE WORD?"

And if they don't know what it is, you don't go with them.

Here is a question you can use to help figure out what your SMART VOICE is saying, and this works in all situations.

All actions have somewhat predictable consequences, and therefore

your SMART VOICE can look into the future...

You try to look ahead, to see what might happen if you listen to this voice, or to that voice.

What you have to ask is, "If I do this, what might happen as a result?" Specifically, ask what is the WORST thing that could happen?

If someone tells you that he has a box of puppies in his car, and you *don't* go over to the car, what is the worst that can happen? Well, you won't get to see the puppies. But so what? That's not so bad.

But ask yourself, if you *do* go over to the car, what is the worst that could happen? Well, the worst that could happen is that the Stranger would grab you and put you in his or her car and take off with you and kidnap you. And that would be terribly, terribly, horribly bad.

So your SMART VOICE would tell you not to go over to the car, because missing out on seeing puppies is way better than getting kidnapped.

It's the same with all the other things we have talked about. If your ball or your bicycle or something else of yours is over next to a car and that is not where you left it, if you don't go get it, what is the worst that could happen? You might lose it, or someone might steal it.

But these things can be replaced, and even if they couldn't, they are NOT more important than YOU, and

you CAN'T
be replaced

If you do go and get them and someone grabs you and steals you away from your family, what you will lose can never be replaced. And what your family will lose can never be replaced.

So listen to your SMART VOICE, and go get a Trusted Grown-Up and tell them what happened. They can get your ball or your bike or your skateboard or your scooter or your toy.

And how about the case of someone who tells you that something terrible has happened and your parents told them to come and get you, and they tell you that your parents didn't have a chance to tell them the FAMILY CODE WORD. What can your SMART VOICE see in the future there?

If you don't go with the Stranger, what is the worst that can happen? If something terrible really has happened, you will find out about it eventually. Meanwhile, there probably wouldn't be anything you could do about it if it was true, so you don't *need* to go anywhere. But if the Stranger was not telling you the truth, the worst that could happen is you could get kidnapped.

Don't ever go with someone who is not one of your Trusted Grown-Ups if they can't tell you the FAMILY CODE WORD, no matter WHAT they tell you. Instead, go and find a Trusted Grown-Up.

Sometimes Strangers might try to fool kids by telling them that their parents don't want them anymore. They say, "Oh, your parents can't afford to take care of you anymore. You know how money has been tight at your house? So they are sending you to live with me now."

Should you ever believe someone who tells you something like this?

??????

NO WAY!

Listen to your SMART VOICE, and it will tell you the truth, that your family loves you, and that they would never, ever send you to live with someone else.

Or a Stranger might tell you that something happened to your parents, so you have to go and live with them.

Should you ever believe someone who tells you something like this?

NO!

Listen to your SMART VOICE, and it will tell you that if anything had happened to your parents, one of your Trusted Grown-Ups would have come along to tell you and take care of you.

Then there are Strangers who might try to get you to go with them, or to stay with them, by telling you that if you don't do it, then something bad will happen

22

to your family. They tell you that if you don't do what they tell you to do, that they will hurt someone you love, or maybe even your pet.

Should you ever believe someone who tells you something like this?

NO, NO, NO!
Strangers who say things
like this are LYING!

People who pick on kids are cowards and liars! They can't hurt your family. Plus, your SMART VOICE will tell you that if you tell your parents about this, they can call the police and have the Stranger person arrested. Then he can't hurt anybody.

There is one thing that kids seem to say all the time. They usually say it when their mom or dad or other Trusted Grown-Up says, "No, you can't do what you want to do or go where you want to go, because it might not be safe."

Then the kid's I WANT voice starts getting upset, and tries to figure out a way to convince the mom or dad or Trusted Grown-Up to let them do what they want.

So they say,

> **IF ANYBODY TRIES TO KIDNAP ME,**
> **I WILL JUST KICK THEM!**

It seems that a lot of kids think that they can beat up a kidnapper and get away.

It is a good thing that kids want to fight. If ever someone does try to kidnap you, you should definitely kick and hit and fight in whatever way you can.

But it is far better to avoid dangerous situations. Grown-ups are stronger than children. If you get close enough for a Stranger to grab you, you will have a very difficult time getting away from him or her. So LISTEN TO YOUR MOM OR DAD OR TRUSTED GROWN-UP. They love you and they want to keep you safe.

There are some times, however, when someone you know turns out to be a Stranger. Your SMART VOICE can tell you if this is happening.

If your SMART VOICE starts whispering to you that what this person is asking you to do doesn't feel right, then don't do it.

If someone you know asks you to go somewhere with them and one of your Trusted Grown-Ups hasn't said it's okay, then don't go. Don't go inside their houses, even if they are right nearby.

And remember, just because you have seen someone lots of times, or even if they live in your neighborhood, that doesn't make them a Trusted Grown-Up unless your parents have told you so, and unless you know they take care of you sometimes.

Don't even go into another room with a person who is not your Trusted Grown-Up if your SMART VOICE is whispering to you.

Don't go ...

Even if you know them, if someone starts making you feel creepy, tell a Trusted Grown-Up.

You don't have to do whatever anyone tells you to do. Just because someone is a grown-up that doesn't make them your boss. Listen to your SMART VOICE. If someone you know seems to be acting like a Stranger, get away from them and tell your Trusted Grown-Up.

GETTING AWAY!

Okay, so what if something goes wrong, and you do get kidnapped by a Stranger. You can still listen to your SMART VOICE, and it can help you save yourself.

If someone ever does kidnap you, you do not have to be a good kid for them. In fact, you should be as bad as you can be. You should SCREAM, and KICK, and HIT them.

Your AFRAID voice is going to be scared. It might tell you to do whatever you are told. It might tell you not to make the Stranger mad because it thinks they will be nice to you if you are nice. But you already know that Stranger is not nice. If they have kidnapped you, you already know that they are bad, bad, bad. So you need to be STRONG, be BRAVE, and FIGHT FOR YOUR FREEDOM!

Because you are smaller than a grown-up, you probably won't be able to beat them up, but there are certain places where they can be hurt easily. It might sound kind of icky, but if you can stick your thumbs or your fingers into their eyeballs, it might hurt them enough that you can get away. Ewwww, gross, I know. But if someone is hurting you and you need to do it to save yourself, you can do it.

Let your SMART VOICE look around where you are, and see what else you might be able to use. If there is anything you can throw into their eyes, it will help you. That could be anything from hot coffee to floor cleaner to dirt. If you can keep them from seeing even for awhile, you can get away.

If the Stranger is driving you in a car, move around as much as you can, thrash, scream. You want to make it hard for them to drive, and you also want to draw as much attention to yourself as you can.

If you can, try to turn the car off and take the keys out. Maybe you can have a Trusted Grown-Up show you how to do this, and you can practice so you will know how to do it.

And if you do get the keys, throw them FAR AWAY. If you can, throw them out the window, as far as you can. At the very least, throw them as far away in the car as you can, into the back seat.

If you are in a car that is driving down the street, you can reach your foot over and push down on the accelerator or brake. You might cause an accident, so you don't want to do it unless you know you are in danger, but usually being in an accident is better than being kidnapped, because if you are in an accident somebody will call the police and you will get help. You should talk to your parents or your Trusted Grown-Ups about this beforehand, and do what they tell you to do, but when you are in danger you need to listen to your SMART VOICE. If you are speeding on the freeway it might be very dangerous to cause an accident, but if you are driving on a city street, it might be better than what the kidnapper has planned.

If ever somebody should put you in the trunk of a car, sometimes you can actually break out the glass in the lights on the back of a car. Then if you do that, stick your hands out and wiggle your fingers. Bang on the trunk if you can. Try to get attention from other cars. Maybe you could have a Trusted Grown-Up show you how you can find the tail lights in the trunk of a car, just so you will know. Some trunks also have a release latch on the inside, so you can ask your Trusted Grown-Up to show you how to find that, and show you how it works. And just so you know, you don't usually need to get into a trunk to see these things. That way you can't even accidentally get locked into one.

If you are ever held captive in a house, try to escape if you can. It is okay to break the windows, or anything else.

Wherever you are, continue to try to get attention. Yell and scream. Flick the lights on and off. Throw things out the windows. Again, let your SMART VOICE look around you and find things you can use. As yourself, "What can I do right here and now with what I have?"

Just remember that what you want to do is:

1. Make everything as difficult as possible for the Stranger. It is okay to hurt them.

2. Try to get the attention of other people and let them know that you need help.

3. Try to get away. It is okay to do whatever you have to do in order to do this, including breaking things.

One really simple thing you can remember is that if someone is holding onto your arm, instead of just pulling away from them, turn your arm and move it towards their thumb. That is an easy way to break their grasp even though they may be much stronger than you are.

If you are able to take a self defense class, they will teach you how to break out of someone's grasp. If you can't take a class, maybe you could practice with your Trusted Grown-Ups so if you ever need to get away from someone who is holding onto your arm, you will know how.

Talk with your Trusted Grown-Ups. Practice "what if" situations so you can give your SMART VOICE practice, and so your Trusted Grown-Ups can help you teach your SMART VOICE.

And most important of all,
have fun and be happy!

You don't have to go around being afraid. Learn to listen to your SMART VOICE, follow the basic safety rules, make sure your parents or Trusted Grown-Ups always know where you are, and make sure you always have permission to be there. And then enjoy your life.

Most people are nice, and most people care about children. There are a few bad people in the world, and they do some bad things to other people, including children. But you can be SMARTER than they are, and that's a pretty powerful thing.

Listen to your Trusted Grown-Ups and do what they tell you to do.

Pay attention to what is around you.

Listen to your SMART VOICE, and stay safe!

COMING SOON!

CHILD SAFETY FOR PARENTS:
How to Keep Your Sanity While Keeping Your Kids Safe
By Sharon Nemeth Murch

This is a companion to Listen To Your Smart Voice, with additional information and suggestions for parents who are concerned for their children's safety in this world today. This book also addresses the changing concepts of safety as children become teens and young adults, and the gradual process of letting go.

MISSING MICHAELA
By Sharon Nemeth Murch

What "The Shack" only imagined, "Missing Michaela" has actually lived. This is the story of the kidnapping of Michaela Joy Garecht, the victim of a witnessed stranger abduction at the age of nine. It has been more than twenty years since Michaela was kidnapped, but although she has not been found, her case has never grown cold, as her family and investigators continue to search for her.

Missing Michaela is also the story of Michaela's mother's emotional and spiritual journey in the years since her daughter's kidnapping, and of the answers she has found to some of the most difficult questions. How could God allow something like this to happen? Why did he not save Michaela? How can we believe in a loving God in the face of the suffering we see in this world?

Please check amazon.com for availability or e-mail
missingmichaela@gmail.com

Acknowledgements

I want to thank Pastor David Silvey of The House church in Mountain House, California (www.thehousefoursquare.org). Your inspiration and support over the years mean more than I can say. May God bless you as you have blessed me.

Thank you to Michelle Spahn, who has been a caring and compassionate source of support, and the very best cheerleader anybody could want.

Thank you to all my friends for putting up with me over the years, and especially to Janet Gillette.

Thank you to the women of the Tuesday Morning Women's Bible Study at Faith Fellowship in San Leandro, California.

Thank you to my husband, Jeff, for your love and support.

And thank you most of all to my children – Alex, Libby, Robbie, Johnna and Ariel – for putting up with my efforts to try to keep you safe.

Still Missing

Michaela Joy Garecht

Kidnapped November 19, 1988
with us forever in our hearts.

♥

ೲ *We love you, Michaela* ೞ

Please see Michaela's story at
www.myspace.com/missingmichaela

contact information
missingmichaela@gmail.com

Hayward Police 1-800-222-3999